LIVES
AND
TIMES

The Wright Brothers

Margaret Hudson

Heinemann Library
Chicago, Illinois

©2001 Reed Educational & Professional Publishing
Published by Heinemann Library,
an imprint of Reed Educational & Professional Publishing,
Chicago, IL

Customer Service 888-454-2279

Visit our website at www.heinemannlibrary.com

Designed by Ken Vail Graphic Design, Cambridge, England
Illustrations by Alice Englander
Printed in Hong Kong / China

05 04 03 02 01
10 9 8 7 6 5 4 3 2

Library of Congress Cataloging-in-Publication Data
Hudson, Margaret, 1955–
     The Wright brothers / Margaret Hudson.
        p.   cm.—(Lives and times)
     Includes bibliographical references and index.
     Summary: A simple introduction to the lives and work of the two
brothers who invented the first engine-driven flying machine.
     ISBN 1-57572-672-6 (lib. bdg.)   ISBN 1-58810-348-X (pbk. bdg.)
     1. Wright, Orville, 1871-1948—Juvenile literature. 2. Wright,
Wilbur, 1867-1912—Juvenile literature. 3. Aeronautics—United
States—Biography—Juvenile literature.   [1. Wright, Orville,
1871-1948. 2. Wright, Wilbur, 1867-1912. 3. Aeronautics—
Biography.] I. Title. II. Series: Lives and times (Des Plaines, Ill.)
TL540.W7H83   1998
629.13'0092'2—dc21   97-51762
     [B]   CIP
                                                                 AC

Acknowledgments
The Publishers would like to thank the following for permission to reproduce photographs:
Austin J. Brown p. 23; Corbis-Bettmann: pp. 18, 19, 20; Chris Honeywell p. 22; Science Museum/Science
and Society Picture Library p. 17; Wright State University Special Collections and Archives p. 21.

Cover photograph reproduced with permission of Hulton Getty and Smithsonian Institute.

Our thanks to Betty Root for her comments in the preparation of this book.

Every effort has been made to contact copyright holders of any material reproduced in this book.
Any omissions will be rectified in subsequent printings if notice is given to the publisher.

Some words are shown in bold, **like this.** You can
find out what they mean by looking in the glossary.

Contents

Part One

Wilbur Wright was born in 1867, near New Castle, Indiana. His brother Orville was born four years later, in 1871, in Dayton, Ohio.

Wilbur and Orville always wanted to know
how things worked. In 1893, when Wilbur
was 25 and Orville was 21, they opened a
shop where they made and fixed bikes.

In 1900, Wilbur and Orville began to think about how to build a machine that could fly. At first they made models of **gliders**. Then they built gliders that were big enough to carry a person.

When they found a flat, windy place to fly them, they tested their inventions. In all, they built and tested three gliders, but they did not fly very high.

Three years later, they added an engine to a **glider**. They called it *Flyer I.* Then, on December 17, 1903, at Kill Devil Hill near Kitty Hawk, North Carolina, Orville took off.

Flyer I, with Orville as pilot, stayed in the air for twelve seconds. Wilbur and Orville kept working. By 1905, only three years later, their newest flyer could stay in the air for 30 minutes.

Everyone was excited by this new discovery. Armies all around the world wanted to see how it worked. So did many other people.

Wilbur and Orville traveled around
America and to Europe giving flying shows.

Wilbur and Orville set up the Wright Company using the money they made from their shows.

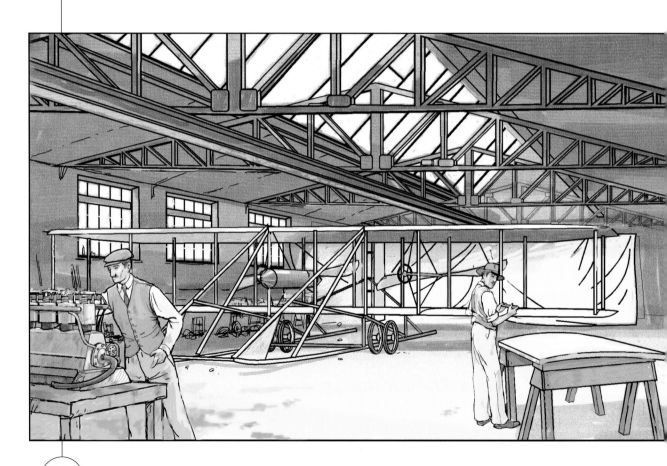

They made flyers to sell. They also taught other people how to fly. They kept making their flyers more powerful and safer.

Wilbur died in 1912, when he was only 45. Orville went on making flyers, which were later renamed airplanes.

Orville's last flight was in 1918. He worked on his airplanes until he died in 1948, at the age of 77.

Part Two

There are many **artifacts** that you can study to learn about Wilbur and Orville Wright.

This is a **replica** of *Flyer I*, the first flying machine powered by an engine. It is in a **museum** in London, England.

Photographs show us what Wilbur and Orville looked like. In this picture they are about 40 years old.

Photographs also show us what early flying machines were like. Can you see the pilot and the wings? How is this airplane different from the airplanes of today?

Newspaper **reporters** at the time wrote about the Wright brothers and their flyers. This newspaper is from 1909, from the Wright brother's **hometown.**

This postcard was made in Germany when Orville visited in 1909. Orville taught a German prince how to fly.

Orville wrote a book called *How We Invented the Airplane*. People can still read it today.

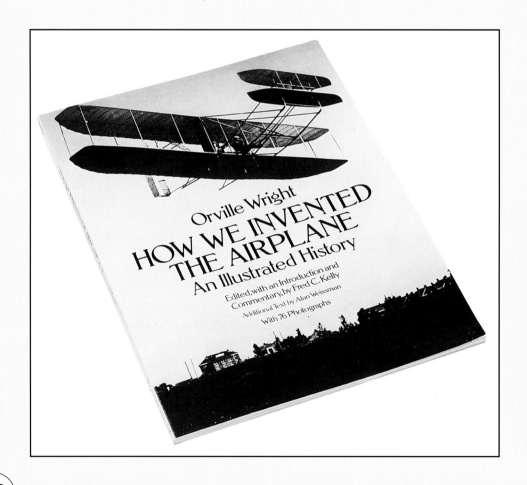

Today, millions of people can travel farther, faster, and safer thanks to the Wright brothers. Airplane builders still use many of the Wright brothers **designs.**

Glossary

artifacts objects made by people, usually from long ago

designs plans that show how something works or is made

glider light airplane without an engine that is kept in the air by the wind

hometown town where a person was born, grew up, or lives

museum place for keeping objects that tell us about how people lived or worked in the past

replica copy of an object

reporters people who write in newspapers

Index

More Books to Read

Kaufman, Mervyn D. *The Wright Brothers: Kings of the Air*. Broomall, Penn: Chelsea House, 1992.

Marquardt, Max. *Wilbur, Orville & the Flying Machine*. Austin, Tex: Raintree Steck-Vaughn, 1989.

Woods, Andrew. *Young Orville & Wilbur Wright: First to Fly*. Mahwah, NJ: Troll Communications, 1992.